BETHLEHEM
IN BROAD
DAYLIGHT

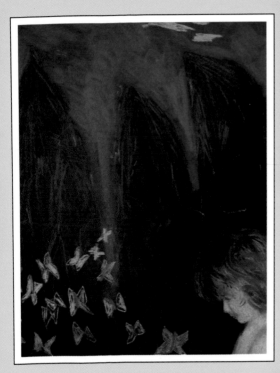

POEMS BY
MARK DOTY

Bethlehem in
Broad Daylight

BETHLEHEM IN BROAD DAYLIGHT

POEMS BY

Mark Doty

David R. Godine, Publisher

BOSTON

First published in 1991 by

DAVID R. GODINE, PUBLISHER, INC.
Horticultural Hall
300 Massachusetts Avenue
Boston, Massachusetts 02115

Library of Congress Cataloging in Publication Data
Doty, Mark.
    Bethlehem in broad daylight / Mark Doty.
      p. cm.
    ISBN 0-87923-848-8
    I. Title.
  PS3554.0798B48   1991
  811'.54—dc20   89-46188

First edition
Printed in the United States of America

For my mother and father

Acknowledgment is made to the following publications, in which some of the poems in this book first appeared:

Agni Review:	"Playland"
	"Six Thousand Terra-cotta Men and Horses"
Calliope:	"*Anna Karenina*"
Crazyhorse:	"Beginners"
	"Cemetery Road"
Dog Pond Review:	"The Ancient World"
Green Mountains Review:	"A Box of Lilies"
Indiana Review:	"63rd Street Y"
Mississippi Review:	"The Garden of the Moon"
New England Review and Breadloaf Quarterly:	"Pharoah's Daughter"
Ploughshares:	"Tiara"
Poetry:	"Ararat"
	"The Death of Antinoüs"
Poetry Miscellany:	"A Collection of Minerals"
Poetry Northwest:	"Adonis Theater"
The Yale Review:	"Harbor Lights"

"Tiara" appeared in *Poets for Life: Seventy-Six Poets Respond to AIDS*, Crown Books, 1989.
"Cemetery Road" appeared in *Spreading the Word*, Bench Press, 1990.

I would like to thank the National Endowment for the Arts for their generous assistance.

Contents

Bethlehem in
Broad Daylight

Harbor Lights

I'm coming home through the red lacquered lobby,
    corridors the bitter green of gingko
        marred by the transoms' milky light.

I am sixteen and the room's three-fifty a night
    in the Chinese hotel on Water Street,
        and I've been out again to the grocery

where they sell cigarettes, one for a dime,
    and to look at the stone face
        in the shop window. I'm calling her

the angel, the mother of angels, and chiseled
    upon the marble of her face is a veil
        so thin it isn't stone at all

but something that emerges out of her chill dreaming.
    It's like watching your mother sleep,
        minutes after you have been conceived,

and her closed eyes say it's all right
    to wake alone, almost at evening, in a city hotel
        where all night from the room next door

comes the sound, I swear, of chopping.
    It's the room of the old woman
        the men at the desk call Mama, and the best

I can imagine is that she's working late
    for the café down the block,
        cleaving celery, splitting the white

and acid green of bok choi. All day
    she'll wash the floors in the halls,
        hissing to herself in sounds I imagine

are curses, damning the residue of the streets
    the residents track all night
        onto the speckled constellations

of the linoleum. She scrubs until it's flawless
    as black water off the piers down the block,
        until the floors gleam green under the window

where RESIDENTIAL shimmers, watery electric
    shantung blossoming over and over
        two stories above the street.

Nights like this, when it's raining
    and the chill seems almost visible,
        coming in across the Sound and the waterfront's

rambling warehouses, the radiator pronounces,
    almost exactly, my mother's name.
        Then the pipes with their silver garlands

sing *runaway*. I've taken the pill I bought
    on the corner, where someone's always reciting
        the litany of an impossible future:

Purple Doubledome, Blue Microdot, Sunshine.
    I'm waiting for the flowers in the cracked linoleum
        to twist and open, scrubbed into blossom,

waiting for the harbor lights
    to burn—the night caught in my hotel window
        like a piece of film in a projector,

melting, so that light comes searing out of the darkness
    first as boiling pinpricks, then a whole angel.
        What I've bought is nothing, aspirin

or sugar, but I don't know that,
    and I'm waiting to come on. It's raining harder,
        the knife in the next room striking

the block, the glass beading up
    and then erasing itself, shimmering the lights,
        and the stone face around the corner

dreams her way out of the world
    of appearances behind her window,
        her glaze of rain, her veil.

Anna Karenina

This morning a hurrying white boat
ripped between the plum tree
and the harbor's rippling sateen;
by afternoon whitecaps break

far out from shore, and gulls reel
by this off-season rental, angels on wires
in a lavish pageant of storm.
Wild grapes scour the roof,

a stunted trunk scrapes
the wet black siding; the wind
investigates anything, like someone
picking through a rummage table

in a terrible hurry. For days
I've grown used to silence;
yesterday I didn't see anyone
but the woman who trundles

every morning toward the canal,
her kerchief flapping blue wings,
her constitutional a bitter duty.
Now the whole house leans

into the wind as she did, and my smoldering fire
and waterjug of sea lavender
seem futile gestures to warm
this summer house pinned to a dune

held by grass and a ribbon of wooden wall.
All day I've been reading *Anna Karenina*,
returning to the chapter in which Tolstoy
brings Anna back to the house in Petersburg,

after the bitter separation, the dawning
awareness that her new lover will not perfect her
after all, when she stands by the bedside
of her son. The boy curls and blinks

out of the deep water of a child's sleep,
lifts himself and then falls,
not back to the pillow, but
into her arms. They had told him

she was dead, but he never believed them,
and though he's falling back
into dream even as he speaks,
he says, "Today is my birthday,

I knew you'd come." Because
she has never stopped longing
for him, she has not imagined
he has grown. And because

the boy can't say what he knows—
that she is perfect and unhappy—
he tells her how he fell on a hill
in the park, and somersaulted three times,

and she forgets to open the bag of toys
she chose the day before. It's dusk,
the storm hardly let up,
but the little triangle of sail

skitters over the water again,
milky gray as the moths that fold
against the windows. How do they hold on?
I can't imagine how cold the sailor

must be, though I can guess
something of his exhilaration—
how the sail must fill and push
against him. I think I might see

the woman in blue making her way
down the shore again, only
to feel that pressure. And the mother
who's lost everything sits on the edge

of the coverlets with such tenderness,
the weight of her son against her, though
she is barely able to be with him at all,
her thoughts are on the future so.

The Ancient World

Today the Masons are auctioning
their discarded pomp: a trunk of turbans,
gemmed and ostrich-plumed, and operetta costumes
labeled inside the collar "Potentate"
and "Vizier." Here their chairs, blazoned
with the Masons' sign, huddled
like convalescents, lean against one another

on the grass. In a casket are rhinestoned poles
the hierophants carried in parades;
here's a splendid golden staff some ranking officer waved,
topped with a golden pyramid and a tiny,
inquisitive sphinx. No one's worn this stuff
for years, and it doesn't seem worth buying;
where would we put it? Still,

I want that staff. I used to love
to go to the library—the smalltown brick refuge
of those with nothing to do, really,
'Carnegie' chiseled on the pediment
above columns that dwarfed an inconsequential street.
Embarrassed to carry the same book past
the water fountain's plaster centaurs

up to the desk again, I'd take
The Wonders of the World to the Reading Room
where Art and Industry met in the mural
on the dome. The room smelled like two decades
before I was born, when the name
carved over the door meant something.
I never read the second section,

"Wonders of the Modern World";
I loved the promise of my father's blueprints,
the unfulfilled turquoise schemes,
but in the real structures
you could hardly imagine a future.
I wanted the density of history,
which I confused with the smell of the book:

Babylon's ziggurat tropical with ferns,
engraved watercourses rippling;
the Colossus of Rhodes balanced
over the harbormouth on his immense ankles.
Athena filled one end of the Parthenon,
in an "artist's reconstruction",
like an adult in a dollhouse.

At Halicarnassus, Mausolus remembered himself
immensely, though in the book
there wasn't even a sketch,
only a picture of huge fragments.
In the pyramid's deep clockworks,
did the narrow tunnels mount toward
the eye of God? That was the year

photos were beamed back from space;
falling asleep I used to repeat a new word
to myself, *telemetry*, liking the way
it seemed to allude to something storied.
The earth was whorled marble,
at that distance. Even the stuck-on porticoes
and collonades downtown were narrative,

somehow, but the buildings my father engineered
were without stories. All I wanted
was something larger than our ordinary sadness—
greater not in scale but in context,
memorable, true to a proportioned,
subtle form. Last year I knew a student,
a half mad boy who finally opened his arms

with a razor, not because he wanted to die
but because he wanted to design something grand
on his own body. Once he said, *When a child*
realizes his parents aren't enough,
he turns to architecture.
I think I know what he meant.
Imagine the Masons parading,

one of them, in his splendid get-up,
striding forward with the golden staff,
above his head Cheops' beautiful shape—
a form we cannot separate
from the stories about the form,
even if we hardly know them,
even if it no longer signifies, if it only shines.

A Collection of Minerals

Weekdays on the island my father
engineered a road past the pink
and blue of empty summer houses
to the missile silo; he took me down once
into the corrugated metal shaft

where the white rocket would be
lowered into place, covered over
with brush and earth once the warhead
was assembled. That afternoon
I reeled in a yellowtail,

a disk of a fish
the color of his bulldozers,
gills fluttering on the narrow body
only my thumb's width from eye
to windshield eye: glittering

fool's gold, no good
to eat. Then, my father intent
on the water, my line rushed in zigzags
like a faultline opening;
what I pulled onto the metal pier

was a rainbowed thrust
of slick muscle coiling
far from anything it knew,
shuddering in air as if
it were in pain, as if

it required secrecy
and darkness. My father ran
to the back of his flatbed
—the government truck, its number
stenciled in a chalky tattoo—

rifled in his toolbox for the machete
he oiled and sharpened Saturday mornings.
This was Titusville, Florida,
the year our class practiced
climbing under our desks,

holding our hands over our faces
and eyes; our mothers stocked up
on canned goods, making caches
beneath the kitchen sink, "in case,"
and men bought knifes or rifles

for "protection." How sad we must have looked,
the fourth grade kneeling
on the marbled linoleum
while our teacher described the sirens,
what would become of the windows,

and offered us the defense
of our formica desktops placed squarely
between ourselves and unimaginable
light. In my mineral collection,
a box of little stones glued in rows

and labeled—feldspar, amethyst,
pyrite—there was a tiny green chunk
of uranium. I'd opened the box
in the dark to see if it would glow
like the face of my parents' alarm,

expecting its chilly radiance
to steal over my bed as it burned out
its half-life. But nothing happened,
and so I kept it in a drawer,
thinking it would change something,

something it touched might become important
or gigantic. When the teacher said
if the bomb fell our bodies would change,
I thought of the jagged surface
of the stone, ancient

and at home in the dark. My father
hacked at the eel until
there were only fragments
of the rippling it had been;
even the pieces

twisted on the steel pier
until he swept them over the edge
with the blade, and told me to pack
my tackle box, and drove me home—
where I was restless, and felt

something had been violated, cut apart
from its submerged privacy,
and the stones in the case seemed puny
and trivial, the sheen of the satin spar
unlikely and disturbing, the uranium

turned inward, revealing nothing,
and in a while I tore the stones loose
from the box one by one and traded them
for something I now cannot remember.

The Garden of the Moon

The school bus rattled around more turns
in the desert roads than I'd ever
be able to trace again, the summer I worked
in Head Start and the lead teacher
arranged a field trip from the barrio
to the Valley of the Moon.

We parked at a high ramshackle fence
straddling a swatch of creosote and mesquite.
There was nothing to the old man
swinging open the gate but shape—
black clothes, black beekeeper's hat—
and as his glove smoothed the veil

he welcomed us, in a sort of stage whisper,
to the Valley of the Moon, *built with the love
and spiritual assistance of many,*
and he led us in. The children walked with partners,
the teacher watching for stragglers or hazard;
I was assigned to Antonio, the boy

she mistrusted most. The path climbed
to shoulder-high alps of cement encrusted
with broken crockery and bits of glass,
junk mosaics capped with figures:
a chipped chalk-ware Snow White gathered
her glittered skirt, looking forward eagerly

from her high-collared cape as if everything
were about to be delivered to her.
At the mouth of a little cave the children
were instructed to dig for treasure;
they kicked till they found pennies in the sand,
and the teacher asked if they were meant to keep them.

The old man told us to speak softly,
if at all, because we were coming
to a place of great serenity,
and he led us down a curving stair
into a two-story grotto he'd hollowed
out of earth; weathered concrete seats

ringed a washtub pool, a mynah bird whispered
in a metal cage. *Whenever you are troubled,*
the old man said, *send your thoughts here.*
The bird spoke a few phrases for us;
even Antonio concentrated on its black sheen,
the old man's gestures. Water dripped

along one wall and I noticed how small
his battered black shoes were
on the ground he'd made himself.
Everywhere around the rim of this one were other,
unfinished gardens, a world of things
he might use to build them. *Your astral body*

can travel to the Garden of the Moon.
Later, in a leaning circus tent filled
with empty cages and Victorian photographs
of fairies, he performed a little lame magic,
which the children liked best,
along with the pennies: bouquets

pulled from sleeves, a dove
from a jiggling hat. The air
would never lift the veil enough
to show his face. At the gate
he'd hand us each a business card
stitched with a scarlet sequin,

printed with the motto, The Key
to the Fairy Treasure House Up,
Up in the Valley of the Moon,
and we'd file onto the bus where
the driver waited, reading a magazine,
and flash our brilliant souvenirs

in the windows all the way home.
But in the magic tent, when a real snake
emerged from a basket and a winged glimmer
slid down a wire and landed in a bloom
of smoke and sparks, Antonio forgot himself
enough to hold my hand, and leaned forward

like the statuette of Snow White,
with that same breathless look.

Isis: Dorothy Eady, 1924

I was never this beautiful.
I don't know if anyone can see how much more
I've become tonight, when the boys
    hired to play Nubians still the peacock fans,
        and another girl and I,

    in simple white robes tied with golden sashes,
perform "The Lament of Isis and Nephthys,"
in the Andrew Long translation:
    Sing we Osiris dead, soft on the dead
        that liveth are we calling.

The scene represents dawn,
and before the painted canvas riverbank
we are kneeling over the void
    left by my husband the God.
        Dorothy, my friend said,

how should I pose? I told her
to bend as though we were mourning
the world's first grief, though of course
    there is no body, since God
        has been torn to pieces

and I am to spend an eon
reassembling him. In the floodlamps
she speaks the text in her best elocution,
    fixed in a tragic tableau,
        and she makes no mistakes,

though she brushes the fringe
of the dropcloth once and for an instant
Egypt ripples. And though this pageant
    on the stage of my father's theatre
        isn't any more than prelude

    to the cinema, I live my role,
the world I remember—I *do* remember—
restored to an uncompromised luster,
    not a single figure defaced
        on the wall of anyone's tomb.

    He *was* my husband,
and I know he had to break apart,
in the ancient world, and tonight,
    so that in thousands of years,
        in the intimacy of dreams,

    the pageant's trance,
I could reconstruct him
bit by bit, like so many shards.
    Anything can be restored,
        even his golden hands.

    There is no time here,
where I am, on the stage of the Plymouth Theatre,
reciting the lament the people used to walk
    from Thebes to Abydos to hear,
        rendered into English verse wrongly,

    though the audience accepts it,
as they always have, and are moved.

Ararat

Wrapped in gold foil, in the search
and shouting of Easter Sunday,
it was the ball of the princess,
it was Pharoah's body
sleeping in its golden case.
At the foot of the picket fence,
in grass lank with the morning rain,
it was a Sunday school prize,
silver for second place, gold
for the triumphant little dome
of Ararat, and my sister
took me by the hand and led me
out onto the wide, wet lawn
and showed me to bend into the thick nests
of grass, into the darkest green.
Later I had to give it back,
in exchange for a prize,
though I would rather have kept the egg.
What might have coiled inside it?
Crocuses tight on their clock-springs,
a bird who'd sing himself into an angel
in the highest reaches of the garden,
the morning's flaming arrow?
Any small thing can save you.
Because the golden egg gleamed
in my basket once, though my childhood
became an immense sheet of darkening water
I was Noah, and I was his ark,
and there were two of every animal inside me.

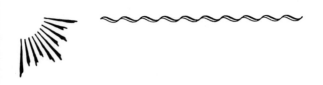

Beginners

The year Miss Tynes enrolled our class
in the Object of the Month Club,
a heavy box arrived each month
from the Metropolitan Museum.
What emerged once—when volunteers
opened each latch, and one lucky girl

lifted the wooden lid away—
was an Egyptian cat, upright on its haunches,
unapproachable, one golden earring flashing,
a carved cartouche between its legs.
Miss Tynes read a translation of the hieroglyphics
and a paragraph depicting the glory

of thousands of mummies ranged on shelves
in the dark—cased and muslined cats,
ibis, baboons—their jewelry ready to offer
any sliver of sunlight back, if it ever touched them.
Later, the cat ruled the back of the room,
fixed on a countertop beside a model

of the planets and a display of moths.
When we'd finished our work it was all right
to go and stand beside it,
even, if we were careful, touch it.
I'd read a story in which two children
drank an emerald medicine from a pharmacy urn

forgot their parents, and understood
the speech of cats. Their adventures were nocturnal
and heroic, and their cat became, I think,
the King of Cats, and was lost to them,
so they drank red medicine from the drugstore urn,
and returned to the human world

of speech. I cried, not for their lost pet
but for the loss of language, and my father
forbade me sad books. Some days, after school,
I'd go to my friend Walter's, and we'd play
a simple game: because he was smaller than me,
though no younger, Walter would be the son.

He'd take off his shirt and sit in my lap;
I'd put my arms around him
and rub his stomach, and he would pretend
to cry or be content, liking my hands.
We were ten, or eight. It's too easy
to think of our game as sex before we knew

what bodies could do, before bodies could do
much. There was something else,
at least for me: the pleasure
of touching what became pure form,
not Walter anymore but the sensation
of skin over supple muscle. I was the heroic

father, I loved—not him, exactly,
with his narrow crewcut head which reminded me,
even then, of a mouse—but the formal thing
he'd become, in his room, with the door closed.
We never changed roles; I was the good lover,
I fathered him. We knew enough to keep

the game private, less out of guilt
than a sense of something exposure
might dilute. It was like the way the children
in my class touched the cat, even talked to it,
hesitantly, beginners in a new language,
maybe imagined it might speak back to us.

Though it was the perfect confidant,
since it could take in anything
and remain calm and black and golden
until it was packed away in the varnished box
to another school, where other children
might lean toward it and whisper,
until it was more ancient, with all it knew.

63rd Street Y

All night steam heat pours
from radiators and up the stairwells
to the thirteenth floor,
and I can't sleep because I know
all the windows are thrown wide open,

a voyeur's advent calendar.
If I lean out the screenless frame
the building's twin flanks yield
banks of lit rectangles above a black courtyard
where a few papers lie completely still,

this warm December. Thirteen dizzying stories
show tonight and any night some blank shades
or black glass, and dozens of interiors—
men all right, mostly not young
or strikingly Christian, though certainly associated.

The nude black man two windows over
is lying in bed, Melchior halfway
through his journey, writing a letter home.
And on the twelfth floor, in my favorite window,
only a little corner holding

the foot of the bed visible,
a pair of strong arms are smoothing
a thin red coverlet so carefully
he must be expecting someone. The scene's
too fragmentary to construct a convincing story,

but he smooths the cloth until
I imagine there's not a single wrinkle
on the scarlet spread blushing
the lamplight so that his arms glow
with the color of intimacy. Even

after I'm tired of watching
there's something all night to wake me:
a pigeon flapping toward the sill
like an awkward annunciation, someone singing
in the alley thirteen floors down

—the Ode to Joy?—curiosity
about the red room a floor below, empty now.
In the park, the lamps' circles shrink
along distant paths beneath intricate trees,
Fifth Avenue luminous in its Roman,

floodlit splendor, and there the hulk
of the Metropolitan, where the Neopolitan angels
must be suspended in darkness now,
their glazed silks dim,
though their tempera skin's so polished

even an exit sign would set them blazing.
I'm sleeping a little then thinking
of the single male angel, lithe and radiant,
wrapped only in a Baroque scrap
sculpted by impossible wind. Because

he's slightly built—real, somehow—
there's something shocking
in his nakedness, the svelte hips
barely brushed by drapery;
he's no sexless bearer of God's thoughts.

Divinity includes desire
—why else create a world
like this one, dawn fogging
the park in gold, the Moorish arches
of the Y one grand Italian Bethlehem

in which the minor figures wake
in anticipation of some unforeseen beginning.
Even the pigeons seem glazed
and expectant, fired to iridescence.
And on the twelfth floor

just the perfect feet and ankles
of the boy in the red-flushed room
are visible. I think he must be disappointed,
stirring a little, alone, and then
two other legs enter the rectangle of view,

moving toward his and twining with them,
one instep bending to stroke
the other's calf. They make me happy,
these four limbs in effortless conversation
on their snowy ground, the sheets

curling into the billows sculptors used once
to make the suspension of gravity
visible. It doesn't matter
that it isn't silk. I haven't much evidence
to construe what binds them,

but the narrative windows
will offer all morning the glad tidings
of union, comfort and joy,
though I will not stay to watch them.

The Death of Antinoüs

When the beautiful young man drowned—
accidentally, swimming at dawn
in a current too swift for him,
or obedient to some cult
of total immersion that promised
the bather would come up divine,

mortality rinsed from him—
Hadrian placed his image everywhere,
a marble Antinoüs staring across
the public squares where a few dogs
always scuffled, planted
in every squalid little crossroad

at the farthest corners of the Empire.
What do we want in any body
but the world? And if the lover's
inimitable form was nowhere,
then he would find it everywhere,
though the boy became simply more dead

as the sculptors embodied him.
Wherever Hadrian might travel,
the beloved figure would be there
first: the turn of his shoulders,
the exact marble nipples,
the drowned face not really lost

to the Nile—which has no appetite,
merely takes in anything
without judgment or expectation—
but lost into its own multiplication,
an artifice rubbed with oils and acid
so that the skin might shine.

Which of these did I love?
Here is his hair, here his hair
again. Here the chiseled liquid waist
I hold because I cannot hold it.
If only one of you, he might have said
to any of the thousand marble boys anywhere,

would speak. Or the statues might have been enough,
the drowned boy blurred as much by memory
as by water, molded toward an essential,
remote ideal. Longing, of course,
becomes its own object, the way
that desire can make anything into a god.

Tiara

Peter died in a paper tiara
cut from a book of princess paper dolls;
he loved royalty, sashes

and jewels. *I don't know,*
he said, when he woke in the hospice,
I was watching the Bette Davis film festival

on Channel 57 and then—
At the wake, the tension broke
when someone guessed

the casket closed because
he was *in there in a big wig
and heels,* and someone said,

*You know he's always late,
he probably isn't here yet—
he's still fixing his makeup.*

And someone said he asked for it.
Asked for it—
when all he did was go down

into the salt tide
of wanting as much as he wanted,
giving himself over so drunk

or stoned it almost didn't matter who,
though they were beautiful,
stampeding into him in the simple,

ravishing music of their hurry.
I think heaven is perfect stasis
poised over the realms of desire,

where dreaming and waking men lie
on the grass while wet horses
roam among them, huge fragments

of the music we die into
in the body's paradise.
Sometimes we wake not knowing

how we came to lie here,
or who has crowned us with these temporary,
precious stones. And given

the world's perfectly turned shoulders,
the deep hollows blued by longing,
given the irreplaceable silk

of horses rippling in orchards,
fruit thundering and chiming down,
given the ordinary marvels of form

and gravity, what could he do,
what could any of us ever do
but ask for it?

Playland

The piano player's straightened hair
gleams wet under a blue spot, and he strikes
up an arpeggio, and everyone up the long
steep stairs at the Playland Café sings:
Pack up all my cares and woes . . .
It is not a café, but a sort of sequin

buried in the smoked skin of a neighborhood
of old leather and garment lofts, soot-stained facades,
the lower floors spangled with peep shows
and arcades, and the neon blinks above the black entry
to the black and raspberry moiré room
where the drag queen behind the piano and a cocktail

gestures the lyrics *No one here can love*
or understand me with one hand,
as if reaching to gather in her audience.
They can, certainly do, and she draws her hand
back toward herself effortlessly, as if
through long habit it no longer requires

even her attention. The black bar, the empty stage
with its tinsel curtains don't ever change,
though the place is spangled for every holiday,
probably nearly single-handedly
keeping the crepe-paper-streamer industry alive—
and tonight it's decked for the Fourth of July,

Miss Liberty's birthday, and the jokes are sweet
and inevitable: Who's carrying the torch,
who's under those skirts, whose legs
are spread in the harbor? The drunk
who wants to bless and marry us
makes the sign of the cross and rambles

in Latin, and though it's silly
it makes me want to stay here all night.
I've never seen anyone but us leave,
and I believe that everyone here
has been dead for years,
and that they not only don't mind

but are truly happy, because here
there is no need to guard themselves,
no possibility of an aesthetic mistake,
and no one is too old, too poor
or mistaken. When the queen walks by
in her black pumps—she must have tried heels

and given up, though somehow her walk
still creates the impression of heels—
she walks for all of us: aerial,
haughty, not bothering to look to either side,
intent on what she's made of herself
and how, and where she's going

—which is only the bar,
draped with bunting, but she might as well
be walking to her own country. Which is this one:
undeniably dangerous and slated,
probably, for demolition, but forgiving;
anyone's taken in, liberties given

to all comers here at the bottom,
where no one wills to come. *Oh,*
everyone does, but would you go home
with anyone here? Besides,
it's early yet. Forgiveness
for her tired hair—her own,

for the black dress accentuating her wide shoulders,
the same rhinestones. It doesn't matter;
another night of artifice is as exhausting
as it is necessary. I hope
she walks forever: that the sign
over the black door keeps pronouncing

its credo, *Playland,* that the piano player,
his voice embalmed in gravel and honey
continues, *Yes, light the light, I'll be home*
late tonight.

Adonis Theater

It must have seemed the apex of dreams,
the movie palace on Eighth Avenue
with its tiered chrome ticket-booth,
Tibetan, the phantom blonde head

of the cashier floating
in its moon window. They'd outdone each other
all over the neighborhood, raising
these blunt pastiches of anywhere

we couldn't go: a pagoda, a future,
a Nepal. The avenue fed into the entry
with its glass cases of radiant stars,
their eyes dreamy and blown

just beyond human proportions to prepare us
for how enormous they would become inside,
after the fantastic ballroom of the lobby,
when the uniformed usher would show the way

to seats reserved for us in heaven.
I don't know when it closed,
or if it ever shut down entirely,
but sometime—the forties?—

they stopped repainting the frescoes,
and when the plaster fell they merely
swept it away, and allowed
the gaps in the garlands of fruit

that decked the ceiling above the second balcony.
The screen shrunk to a soiled blank
where these smaller films began to unreel,
glorifying not the face but the body.

Or rather, bodies, ecstatic
and undifferentiated as one film ends
and the next begins its brief and awkward exposition
before it reaches the essential

matter of flesh. No one pays much attention
to the screen. The viewers wander
in the steady, generous light washing back
up the long aisles toward the booth.

Perhaps we're hurt by becoming
beautiful in the dark, whether we watch
Douglas Fairbanks escaping from a dreamed,
suavely oriental city—think of those leaps

from the parapet, how he almost flies
from the grasp of whatever would limit him—
or the banal athletics of two or more men who were
and probably remain strangers. Perhaps

there's something cruel in the design
of the exquisite plaster box
built to frame the exotic
and call it desirable. When the show's over,

it is, whether it's the last frame
of Baghdad or the impossibly extended
come shot. And the solitary viewers,
the voyeurs and married men go home,

released from the swinging chrome doors
with their splendid reliefs
of the implements of artistry,
released into the streets as though washed

in something, marked with some temporary tatoo
that will wear away on the train ride home,
before anyone has time to punish them for it.
Something passing, even though the blood,

momentarily, has broken into flower
in the palace of limitless desire—
how could one ever be *done* with a god?
All its illusion conspires,

as it always has, to show us one another
in this light, whether we look to
or away from the screen.

A Row of Identical Cottages

All night the flag outside our window
rippled above wet lilacs and someone's motorbike
    parked on the guest-house lawn.

At dawn I watched the houses lean
and crowd toward the pier, picket fences tumbling,
    the roses akimbo. Then the cycle

stuttered, the flag flapped
like a towel hung out to dry
    —starry field fading—and the sheet

covering your chest broke like the sea's
own banner, an edge-line of foam
    on a dark shore. I didn't want to wake you.

That day—years ago—we drove
by a row of cottages just above the beach.
    We didn't stay, or even stop,

but I can still see that line
of white clapboard boxes, barely big enough
    for a bed, each bearing a wooden sign

stenciled in green paint:
their names, which marched from *Aster*
    to *Zinnia*, a floral alphabet.

Traveling brings back every other summer
by the sea; our long, familiar conversation's
    all *I remember* . . . and *Then* . . .

Memory seems a kind of shoreline,
the edge between sleep and the world.
    We're never sure what we'll wake to—

    what form the past, which has no boundaries,
has chosen for its intrusion into today,
    or how our random memories will match

    or collide. Remember Nantasket Beach,
on Labor Day, and how the Polish band
    pumped out songs for the dancers,

    old men and women bused
from the housing project? They held one another
    as if they'd never let go,

    and in the roofless bathhouse
you remembered your mother's angular
    white sunglasses, the waxy pink sticks

    for fixing Polaroids, I my father's Kodak
and old blue trunks; the details
    don't matter, only the intimacy

    they carry with them. Did I ever tell you
this? One summer vacation day it rained,
    and I must have been allowed out alone;

    I remember discovering a ladder
beside the shore, stark by the single
    breathing undulance that sea and sky made.

A gull perched on top, triumphant
over a crust, his weight perched
        on one leg, then the other.

        Someone—a lifeguard?—must have lugged
the ladder out, abandoned it
        beside the water that was hurrying

        with the idea of storm. Nothing happened,
but the image is as clear as if
        I could mount the wooden steps.

        Every year we drive to the beach
as if we needed something huge
        but almost apprehensible,

        its only containment the line
that moves back and forth along blank sand,
        blurring the shore. Only a little

        and indefinite border, the line
between then and now, the foamy edge-line
        where my ladder stood. Five years ago

        in that rented room I saw the shoreline break
above your heart, and that was all the dazzled coast
        I could want or hold. I could never remember

        so much alone. I think of that garden row
of cottages as a code for summer:
        the names of flowers marking, regular as iambs,

the blank verse of a beach motel.
Not a place we'd ever want to stay
    (who could choose between *Marigold* and *Dahlia*?)

    but an image to keep, like a snapshot
acquiring the creased signatures
    of long attention. Not flowers,

    exactly, but words, all we can climb to,
stenciled on the clapboard along the waterfront:
    Cleome, Peony, Rose.

A Box of Lilies

I'm driving to work, late,
Tannhauser on the tape player—

the skittering violins spiraling down
in their mortal pull

while the horns play out their grand theme:
the brilliant flourishes

before they fall. The strings plummet
again and again, and then the student

I'm meeting tells me he's fallen
in love, an old girlfriend

still lingering somewhere, the new sleek
with possibility. It doesn't matter

so much, he says, which he winds up loving;
his fall's "a beautiful event

with no significance." There's something bravura,
something nineteen in even saying it,

and I can't decide whether
to love or blame him, thinking of you,

how yesterday morning you set out
on a kind of going

we don't know the least thing about.
If I'd known you better I couldn't even

say this. This is what I imagine it's like,
Doug: once the mailman brought me

a box of lilies, by mistake
—shipping error, nursery packer's

benevolent whim?—
twenty-eight pale and armored hearts,

spiky as artichokes.
Nothing was labeled

but I could guess their intentions
by their heft; some were twinned,

even two-fisted, and the instructions plain:
Dig deeper than you need to.

fertilize with a little bone,
allow to remain undisturbed

for years. It took me a moment
to decide to keep them,

seasons to watch the stalks
thicken, the sure swell

of buds into waxy throats. My neighbor
leans down from her dizzying

third-floor porch, July,
toward the advent of trumpeting;

it's the beautiful event
in the garden she waits for,

and their fragrance goes hurrying
up; she's an interruption

en route to heaven. Last night
I burned two cones of incense

for you, one mesquite, one pine,
then I cleaned the guest room,

spreading a good quilt, arranging flowers.
There wasn't anything else

to do. Maybe dying's like being given
a box of what will be trumpets,

maybe it feels like a mistake,
and you plant them with all

the requisite attention
and wait for something

flaring. In the opera
Else renounces her life for love,

and the truth is her gesture matters
not because it's rare

but because there's nothing else to do
against the way these violins

seem to want to take us,
and will, though not before the horns

have played something unforgettable.
I don't know which I love better—

knowing the bulbs are there, this March,
scaled sleepers, or the brief July spangle

smudging our faces
with that golden lipstick.

I couldn't choose between them,
finally—the downward longing,

the trumpets in their brave clusters
year after year.

Paradise

James L. White, 1936–1981

1.

For you it's a hotel whose prime is long past,
so you don't have to anticipate anything.
All the clerks are beautiful,

and the old details there still:
portals of marble and uranium,
the tragic stones, carved with the forms

of flowers. You've probably named them:
Snowdrift, *First Time*, and one you call
Too Soon, and twisting among them

are the urgent torsos of gods
and horses. Jim, when I was a child
my parents used to take me

to a reconstructed temple,
a museum of broken friezes
where marble horses flared

their nostrils, reared back
as if in horror. For me
they were entirely without context,

the arching necks and huge blind eyes.
They looked as if they'd fling themselves
from their pedestals, contorted

but motionless, as men sometimes are,
in the ferocity of their repose.
I wish I'd known you. I imagine

an endless scrim of snow falls
outside your rented paradise,
though the banks grow no higher;

the downtown street's lovelier
as you grow more oblivious to it,
lost in the shy weight of an Indian boy

who's driven all night from a reservation
in South Dakota. He's going to stay
with you as long as you want. Tonight

you don't have to do anything,
only sleep a little
so that you can wake

to those astonishing flanks again.
Or, heaven is somewhere you don't need
to love anyone to feel all right.

2.

I read that blind children,
in a room painted deep blue,
became more tranquil, at ease,
as if what they could not see their way to
informed them. It's the same
with longing; finally it delivers
the object of desire not into our hands
but into the skin itself,
the bruising tattoo of *I want*.
It isn't even a question,
whether the subject or object
of desire is made more beautiful.

3.

I forget who told the story
about the garden for the blind,
how they'd learn to read the blue
and white rockets of delphinium,

the smolder of larkspur. It makes me
think of the men I used to meet
in the Victory Gardens' drifts
of plots and hedges, every alcove

alive with men until after dawn.
There are only a few I can remember
individually: the shirtless,
rippling boy in the painter's cap,

who was no boy at all,
his face preserved,
I guess, by the force of desire;
Rafael, the Puerto Rican exotic dancer

of the holy namesake, who became
a janitor in the baths,
a job for an angel of strong constitution;
the man who inhaled Freon all night

perched on an abandoned car seat
until he proclaimed himself Queen of the Fens
and fell over backward into the swamp.
Mostly they're vague, downtown lights

hazing above them as they paced
territories fenced by lathe and vine
and flowers that opened in the dark,
face up, throats wide to the moon.

Once the vice squad careened in,
headlights blaring at the only exit
to a little cul de sac and all of us leapt
terrified over the fences; I fell flat

in someone's lettuces, fleeing
the legislation of the body.
I want to defend us now,
our alliance of strangers,

but I don't have to explain it to you,
Jim, the tentative equality of the dark,
the pleasure of banning privacy,
touching anyone you wanted.

Some were too drunk to even stand,
and some just stood as if
they'd forgotten why they'd come.
I didn't know whose hands were whose;

the breathtaking fall from self
brought us farther into the garden,
blind readers who disappeared,
for a while, into the text.

In little clearings half a dozen men
become no one, and lost nothing.
I don't want to glorify this; the truth is
I wouldn't wish it on anyone,

though it is a blessing,
when all your life you've been told
you're no one, and you find a way
to be what you have been told,

and it's all right.

Maybe the dead look back
to the watered green silk of Earth
and name it Desire's Paradise,

and it must be hard for them,
formed as they were once in desire
and then over and over again.

Imagine it's longing that compels them
back to the world. You are snowdrift,
marble, classical in the stasis

in which you die into yourself again,
you feel so complete. Suppose
you have everything you need,

and then you realize what you lack
is need. And so I want you to wake again,
in longing, like the rest of us.

An Exhibition of Quilts

Necessity bloomed
into an exuberance of scraps,

with a rapturous language to match:
Feathered Star with Wild Goose Chase,

Princess Feather with Laurel Leaves,
Unnamed Pattern with Four Hearts.

Four Leaf Sprays and Four Pineapples.
The terms of their craft became landscape:

Prickly Path, Garden Maze,
Delectable Mountains.

Here everything's in motion
—Tumbling Blocks, Carpenter's Wheel—

and here, in one perfected yellow firmament,
are sixteen stars. Some shine

while others spin, since the maker's
shot five through with red plaid

pinwheel blades. The color's softened,
though it must have dazzled.

Which were her dresses,
which her husband's shirts?

Imagine her cutting apart
anything discarded

into squares and diamonds,
hurrying to fit them all in,

to get it right:
just beyond the day's veil,

her gospel's variable heavens.
Did she name it—

Whirling and Sleeping Stars,
Bethlehem in Broad Daylight?

Six Thousand Terra-cotta Men and Horses

Some farmers digging a well
five kilometers outside of Xian
broke through into the tomb,
and corrosive daylight fell

onto the necks of the horses,
the men's knotted hair,
after their dynasties in the dark.
The rooms had been studded

with torches of seals' fat,
so these eyes could, even buried,
give back light. What did the Emperor expect
when the oiled strips of silk

were consumed, smoldering?
The guards were individuated by the sculptors
—whoever *they* may have been—
down to an idiosyncratic chin, the detail

of a frown. This one 192 centimeters tall,
this 186. "Life-size," the catalog says.
Were they portraits, each someone recognized
once, lively and exact? They ranked

in squadrons, self-contained, at rest.
Did the chamber smell of scorched fat still?
And to bury even horses, these animated faces
who look eager to step out onto the wide,

grassy fields outside of Xian.
Their breed is still raised in Quinghai;
the colors incinerated by daylight
must have made them less alien, less formal.

Muscular, monumental as coffins set on end,
they are patient and eager at once,
poised as if beginning the first step
of a purely ornamental journey,

sun on their backs, nothing at stake,
the provinces united years ago
under the Emperor's beautiful will,
which came to nothing, though his horses stared

into the dark perfectly for two thousand years,
good-natured, their faces open and uncomplicated.

Pharoah's Daughter

   The youth groups have all built floats
for the Fourth, and they parade
around and around the green;
    one club's done Pharoah's Daughter
      Finds Baby Moses in the Bullrushes.
      Reeds nailed to the flatbed rattle in the breeze

   while the handmaidens,
bored with their supporting roles,
fan themselves with peacock fans;
    in the blue paper swell cut
      to suggest the edge of the Nile
      a basket bobs a little as the truck bounces.

   In Vacation Bible School
the teacher used to show us pictures,
large, archaic things, from a folio
    I think called *Heroes of Bible Days.*
      They were colored like nothing else,
      lurid and a little unworldly,

   as if to suggest that Bible stories
took place on other planets;
Expulsion from the Garden,
    Joseph and His Coat of Many Colors
      might have been the names of so many stars.
      In the plate representing Pharoah's daughter,

the princess wore a white sheath
out of de Mille, and stood with her arms
thrown back in a theatrical pose
    of astonishment, though her eyes,
        outlined in streaks of kohl, were without surprise,
        simply acknowledging the inevitable arrival

of the child she'd lift from the river.
We knew the boy would be safe from flood,
that the basket wouldn't snag in reeds;
    of course the mild current would always float him
        directly to the place where she was bathing.
        After the story we'd go to the table

and draw, domesticating the exotic landscape
with our own personable, crayoned houses,
smoke twisting from our slanting chimneys.
    And each of us must have seen ourselves
        floating toward our mothers
        across a great distance, wondrous children,

nearly unknowable. Someday our parents
would remember this about us:
that we traveled effortlessly,
    from far over water, an Egypt.
        We might be prophets. And then
        they might stand in that same pose of wonder,

like this high-school girl
chosen to portray her, bent in the same
expected attitude, wobbling a little
    as the truck slows down then lurches around the square,
        looking down, as she has for hours, into the basket
        in which she must imagine the form of her son.

Art Lessons

Bored with the still life her painting teacher
has composed—Oaxacan vase and copper
bowl, ragged sunflowers—my mother takes a long scrap
of watercolor paper and sketches whatever

emerges first: five Chinese horses,
each a few quick strokes of black ink.
Sun on their fluid and restless shoulders,
they seem to be running out her sudden rebellion.

She'll never paint like this again,
though the future doesn't matter now, not while these five
unstoppable animals—angry, perfect—derive
their strength from refusal and hurry off the page.

This isn't the lesson, the art teacher says,
and likes the painting anyway.

∼

What if she'd continued that sheer
pleasure of refusal? No bruised years?
No little paintings of dark and smoldering
lilacs again and again, no vodka blurring

every afternoon to a troubled sheen?
No ice and then no glass: a disease.
Do I still believe that will alone
could have cured her? No one was home,

the world was slick, slurred. Everything's erased,
purposefully forgotten, impossible now to read.
Twenty years and still it's hard to breathe.
Could I let it in, all I still can't say?

That's the lesson: art is remembering, and turning away.
And the poem, refused, hurries off the page.

∼

The sets of slides my parents ordered
came wrapped in beautifully marbled
paper. Projected on our largest wall,
heat from the bulb rippling the image a little,

they offered worlds: a Rennaissance prince taut and alien
as his hawk; breath, in a Botticelli, blooming
into the millefiori of spring; Tintoretto's
palpable silk. When my father questioned Caravaggio's

—boy, was he, lavish hair and ambiguous smile framed
with grapeleaves?—I felt a sense of shame,
though I couldn't have said why.
I was to learn to name the art,

though the lesson ran deeper: this resonant intelligence,
this order, couldn't have come from people like us.

Didn't my parents see that?
We lived in a tract house, in Tucson,
Arizona, and I never heard anyone say *marbled*
or *Veronese*. I liked to stand

in the blasted grass of the backyard and study,
through my father's binoculars, the lavender bulk
of the mountains, the two sharp spires in the cleft
of one peak I thought of as a cathedral,

the shadowy place beneath them a door.
We'd take Sunday drives into the desert
and I saw remnants of some age grander than ours
in every wind-turned pinnacle,

as if the desert were classical,
demanding, framed. I wanted a world

constructed to be read, with an arch,
a tiny human figure in one corner to lend meaning
or scale. I didn't know art
was a world lost from the very beginning.

Now my mother's buried in a desert cemetery
irrigated into lawn, dominated
by the unforgettable outline of those mountains. My family
was a ruined gesture, a building that collapsed,

a few years after the art lessons,
into brutality and incoherence.
I wished myself no one's
son, uncompromised, airy as the monuments

magnified over the Naugahyde sofa, with no context
to embrace or erase. When I visited my father last

we drove to the Grand Canyon, with his new wife,
who has made him happy, and who narrated
every bit of landscape along the way.
And watching the foreign, arid cliffs, it was just the same,

as if I knew something my parents did not: what lay
around us had only been mistaken
for random stones. On a narrow spar over the canyon's
terrifying layers of color, I imagined

I was surrounded by ruins, doors
carved with the reliefs of their vanished inhabitants, doors
that yet would open, if only we could find them,
onto hidden chambers, the heartbreakingly

perfect collonades. Mother, Father,
listen: I was not born but made.

Cemetery Road

No one's been buried here for years,
on this hill above the landing strip
where lovers park, nights, and watch
what few small planes come and go—
maybe they love each other more,
witnessing these ordinary departures.

The evergreens are overgrown,
and the fence just a half-hearted gesture.
A few of the thinner slates—
dark today because it's rained
all morning, the sky hovering
at the edge of the second snow—

are smashed to pieces, a few
worn illegible. Those that stand
lean together in clusters,
stone archipelagos: *Glory*
with all her lamps shall burn . . .
Weep not for me,

I've quit my house of clay . . .
There's no narrative here—
only sentimental or cautionary verses
under the incised urns and willows,
the winged, weeping faces—
but I wanted to tell you this story:

Once I watched a psychic healer
draw pain out with such neutrality,
the way one pulls a weed sometimes,
finding it neither ugly nor beautiful,
merely noting its presence
where it isn't wanted. She told me

to imagine the garden within myself,
inviolable, and asked me to invite
into that brilliant shade
the women who had comforted me:
my grandmother with her red-lettered Bible,
my mother, on her good days.

And when she told me to divide
my own memory, and banish
the darker mother from the garden
I could not, because wherever she was
she was wrapped in a long healing,
and it was all right now.

But the psychic said,
"There is no time there.
All of the story happens at once;
bar her from the garden."
And when I finished the work,
the others who had come to be healed

held me while I was, for a time,
the purely vulnerable child again.
For days I felt furrowed and broken, and doubted
anything had happened at all
but the recurrence of my own grief.
I was wrong. I can't explain

how I know the dead continue,
how sometimes we carry them
and sometimes they propel themselves
into huge distances they understand
only a little better than we do.
And whatever injured me, Mother,

I want to tell you that childhood
is only a little blue grave now.
See, the boy beneath this slate
was born in 1798, and lived a single day,
but anyone walking here one hundred
and eighty-nine years has read his name.

And my own death is only a minor island,
and I will go past it, as you have.
Perhaps you prepare it already,
as one readies a room for guests:
here the clean linens, here
a porcelain bowl. Why did we ever stop

burying beloved objects, the things
found in tombs: toys, jewelry, roses?
What did that child have time
to love, descending into this chilly ground
before his mother's hands
even came into focus? And because

there is no time there,
you are also here with me,
ten years gone and walking
these ruts in the cemetery road,
the wind smelling of new snow
and October, gathering in a rush

under the stiff wings carved
on these blackened stones.
They lift you with such force and grace
I would never think of calling you back.
You are going forward into your future,
though perhaps what lies before you
can't be called that.

Against Paradise

Past the paperwhites breathing
at the window the fence pickets
syncopate my view, a rhythm
off a little, since the skewed posts
lean. It's a good fence,
sturdy despite its eccentricities,

like the neighborhood. The shadowed clapboard
of the apartment house next door's
gone glacial silver, and the pine
concentrates shadow at its core.
Twilight blues the spaces
between the pickets first;

the white spears shine
as footsteps shuffle past
—the paperboy, in his hooded sweatshirt
six-o'clock-in-December blue.
He bounces a kickball on its way
to flat, and in the hush that follows

a neighbor calls from her porch,
which blazes like an altar
of light bulbs and frozen laundry,
Johnny Boy, Johnny Boy,
a name she repeats mysteriously
and at regular intervals,

always in the same tone
which makes me suppose her cat
hasn't been home for years.
All we have of our neighbor's lives
is noise, and the stories we can make of it.
The woman next door goes by

singing, something like *Oh
I'm going to the store
to buy some bread 'cause we don't have any
the roof of my apartment looks
so black* . . . The words meander
around the scale like someone lost,

then fade. She'll be back soon,
wheeling a shopping cart from the grocery
as though it were a gift
she was bringing to the sure location
of a miracle, as though it were her job
to hurry home and continue

this composition of isolated events,
ordinary and fraught with evidence
of how things vanish before we're ready
—the ghost of Johnny Boy
stalking the winter birds—how light
makes things look a certain way

once. Another song to no audience,
then the red cart
abandoned on a sidewalk ranged
with snow, gleaming in last light
as if someone has polished it spotless.
Galaxies of frozen breath,

these narcissus cluster.
The fence literally glows.
I couldn't have imagined that.
Its shadows spike the snow;
I couldn't love any world but this.
It's almost dark. *Johnny Boy.*

About the Author

Mark Doty's first book, *Turtle, Swan* was published by Godine in 1987. His work has appeared in *Poetry, Ironwood, The Yale Review, Ploughshares, Crazyhorse* and other magazines. He has held fellowships from the Vermont Council on the Arts, the Massachusetts Artists Foundation, and the National Endowment for the Arts, and has taught at Goddard College, the MFA Writing Program at Vermont College, and at Sarah Lawrence College. He lives in Provincetown, Massachusetts.

A Note on the Type

BETHLEHEM IN BROAD DAYLIGHT was set in Sabon, a typeface designed by Jan Tschichold. The roman is based on a font engraved by Garamond and the italic on a font engraved by Granjon, but Tschichold introduced many refinements to make these models suitable for contemporary typographic needs. It was set by PennSet, Inc., Bloomsburg, Pennsylvania, and printed by Maple-Vail Book Manufacturing Group, Binghamton, New York.